DEFEATING YOUR GOLIATH

Slaying the Giants in Your Life Starts with You

Karina Camille Davis

WESTBOW® PRESS
A DIVISION OF THOMAS NELSON
& ZONDERVAN

WestBow Press books may be ordered through booksellers or by contacting:

WestBow Press
A Division of Thomas Nelson & Zondervan
1663 Liberty Drive
Bloomington, IN 47403
www.westbowpress.com
1 (866) 928-1240

ISBN: 978-1-4908-8138-6 (sc)
ISBN: 978-1-4908-8137-9 (e)

Library of Congress Control Number: 2015908061

Print information available on the last page.

WestBow Press rev. date: 06/09/2015

To my loving parents Lenord and Rosemary whom have always provided me with an unconditional love that is far beyond explainable, and raised me with the foundation of knowing the love of Jesus Christ. To my two beautiful sisters Lendria and Shantavia my best friends whom I love dearly for always being there. Much love to my brother-in law Lincoln Sr. and my nephews Lincoln Lenord and Lathan Lorenzo who keep me smiling.

I would also like to thank all my family and friends for their words of encouragement. You all have encouraged me to bounce back from every difficulty I have faced. With you all by my side, I realize I never stand alone, and I have a voice in this world. I can stand proud with my feet planted firmly and be heard. To all my brothers and sisters in Christ who are facing, or have ever faced a Goliath in their lives-with Christ you are victorious! To those suffering with Lupus or any illness, to God be the glory in the midst of it all. He will never leave you alone; whatever His plan may be, continue to praise Him through it all.

Press In and Press On

I press in, and I press on
Although looking back a time or two
I still press on, when I can't even see what's in front of me
I refuse to stop even if I must feel my way through
I press in, and I press on
When there seems to be nothing but darkness and I am stumbling around in nightfall
I press on, and follow that still small voice of The Father
Because God is light and there is no darkness in Him at all (1 John 1:5 NLT).
I press in, and I press on
Despite of not knowing what lies ahead
I still press on, though the road most traveled seems safe; it's broad; and it's wide
I choose life; and take the way to kingdom blessings; the narrow road instead
I press in, and I press on
At times my feet may get stuck along the muddied paths of confusion, fear and doubt
I still press on, even if I have to wiggle a little here and wiggle a little there
Then fall down on my knees and pray, "Lord please help me free myself out!"
I press in, and I press on
Never giving up and giving in to struggle and strife
I still press on, moving towards the light keeping my eyes fixed on Jesus, because He is the way, the truth and the life (John 14:6 KJV).
I press in, and I press on
When faced with climbing the highest mountains; or whether face down in the dirt
I still press on in spite of it all; for I know God has an inheritance for me

I just know in my gut, He is about to show Himself strong in the midst of my hurt!
I press in, and I press on
For no weapon formed against me shall prosper; because my God is a consuming flame
I press on; and victory I claim because the battle is already won
Hallelujah! Thank you Jesus, You have added persistent and resilient warrior to my name.

By: Karina Camille Davis

CONTENTS

Introduction xi

Chapter 1   Who Is Goliath? 1
Chapter 2   Leaving Home Fully Dressed for Battle...........................5
Chapter 3   Waist Tightened with the Belt of Truth 7
Chapter 4   Breastplate of Righteousness 11
Chapter 5   Putting on Your Spiritual Shoes...........................15
Chapter 6   Shield of Faith..20
Chapter 7   Helmet of Salvation 26
Chapter 8   Sword of the Spirit 30
Chapter 9   Seeing through the Eyes of God..........................35
Chapter 10 Get a New Mindset...40

INTRODUCTION

"My momma always said, —"'Life is like a box of chocolates. You never know what you're gonna get.'" This is a famous quote by Tom Hanks' character in the award-- winning movie *Forrest Gump* in 1994. I think this quote became famous because it is a very good description of life's unpredictability. If you take a box of chocolates without looking at any names and just blindly pick a piece, you can get a piece that is very delightful or one that's not. Life can sometimes come with an assortment of surprises. The challenges we face in life are things in our lives we just wish we could choose to leave untouched, pick around or just simply avoid.

We have to realize we don't have to choose to live life alone and walk around blindly making choices. We have our Father in heaven that is willing and ready to guide us through the winding roads of life. He is our tour guide, our moral compass, and more importantly, our savior. If we let Him into our lives wholeheartedly, we can come to know the faithfulness of His love. This book's purpose is to help you through the fights of life. I am hoping it will enable you to embrace the faithfulness of God in every area of your life and to know that He will never leave you nor forsake you.

Trusting and knowing God will give us the right tools and armor to battle the giants in our lives. We can never be promised that we won't have a Goliath or— Goliaths—but, defeating them and moving forward starts with you!

CHAPTER 1

WHO IS GOLIATH?

So just who or what is Goliath?

In the Old Testament, book of 1 Samuel, chapter 17 there is an infamous story about a young shepherd boy by the name of David. In the previous chapter, God sent Samuel to anoint David the next King. When Samuel arrived, He took one look at Jesse's son Eliab, and he thought for sure Eliab was the Lord's anointed because of his outward appearance. However, God spoke to Samuel and said, "The Lord doesn't make decisions the way you do! People judge by outward appearance but the Lord looks at a person's thoughts and intentions."

So, Samuel looks at all of Jesse's seven sons the same way, and God rejects all of them. Jesse then sent for David to return from the fields where he was watching the sheep. Young David was small in stature and didn't look as if he would be a great or mighty king. However, God told Samuel, "Arise, anoint him: for this is he" (1 Samuel 16: 12 KJV). From that day forward the Spirit of the Lord was with David. —God knew David was big at heart although he didn't look like a big and mighty warrior. God is not interested in what is on the outside but the inside. He was chosen by God because of his inner man—his, thoughts and intentions. David was a man after God's own heart.

We all should work on our inner spirit more than our outer appearance. As Christians, the Holy Spirit is living on the inside of us. The word of God should be a reflection of our selves. It should reflect in the way we react, respond and handle situations. It should also mirror how we interact with others.

The climax of the story begins when the Israelites and the Philistines are at war. The main villain of the story is the Philistine warrior by the name of Goliath. Goliath stood over nine feet tall! Goliath's large appearance, his resume as a champion, and his cockiness made him very intimidating. Today, we may not have gargantuan men roaming the streets, but we do have modern day situations that seem to tower over us like a giant. We can take this story and compare it to the challenges we face.

For example, there was a time in my life that I felt like problems were just piling on and on. There was always something to deal with before I could even get past the first thing. The month after I finalized my divorce I was diagnosed with Systemic Lupus. I was weighed down with emotional and financial bondage. Before I could learn to cope with all of that I began facing health issues.

Technically, the trials and tribulations I was going through didn't have physical human characteristics but those things alone felt like a giant as intimidating as Goliath. My Goliath was this new found disease I knew nothing about, my failed marriage and all the emotional baggage that followed. I was a complete mess emotionally! I was suffering from depression and anxiety. I was at a point in my life that I was broken. I felt I was defeated and there was no way I would get past the pain. In the midst of my storm I could see no happiness or way out. I am sure this is exactly how the Israelites may have felt. When you are in the midst of your own storm and troubles is when your vision becomes the most myopic.

If we could just learn to be more like David and focus on how big our God is instead of how big the problem is. This helps us to be more positive and can also lessen the amount of time we are in our storm. Just as all the other Israelites were looking at the problem and becoming afraid, I was doing the same thing. I was looking at my situation and not God! The lesson God wanted to teach is that no matter how big our problem— even a giant like Goliath— it, is not bigger than our God! I had to grow, mature and learn from my experiences but not young David. David was fearless from the very beginning.

David answered Goliath's challenge and equipped himself with five stones and,—a sling, but most importantly he had the Lord God Almighty with him. He faced Goliath without any fear despite of Goliath's intimidating appearance and reputation as a champion warrior. David told Goliath that the God of the Israelite armies would defeat him, and He didn't need fancy weapons to succeed. That day Goliath, the giant that tormented all of Israel, was knocked to the ground by one stone from David's sling; and the sword from Goliath's own side.

Do you think that a young, small shepherd boy could have defeated Goliath with only a rock and sling without God's presence? No, of course not! This is a wonderful assurance to us today. God will fight your enemies and even your battles, just as He promised (Joshua 23:10 NLT). David believed this promise and had faith and confidence that God was with him. We need to learn to have the same faith young David had within him. We need to realize that we can overcome anything and know that God will guard the feet of His saints (1 Samuel 2:9 NKJV).

God is omnipotent, omnipresent, and omniscient. We serve a God that literally just spoke the world into existence. God is the same yesterday and today. He does not change. So we can be assured the same God David served is the same God we serve and worship today.

So, why shouldn't we look at our problem as just a mere obstacle that our Lord is greater than? David saw Goliath as nothing more than just that. His faith in the Lord Almighty was bigger than even a giant. He didn't let what he was seeing with his eyes cause him to accept defeat as the others did. He was willing to trust in God, the unseen. Most importantly, when the obstacle seemed too big to overcome, David didn't give up. He fought through it. No problem of any kind is too big for our God to handle. He is bigger than broken hearts and relationships, messed up finances, health concerns, hopelessness, and even rejection. I experienced some of this first hand, so I know he can keep you encouraged until you are delivered from your circumstances. He can do the same thing for you! He is an exceptional God, a deliverer and restorer. You may not have suffered from some of the problems I mentioned, but we all have faced something that has kept us from receiving and believing in God's best for us.

The battle of thoughts in our own minds is like an attack from the enemy. At times it can seem like the biggest giant of them all— WWI and WWII all together! It is the most deceptive tactic of the enemy. The Bible tells us in Ephesians 6:12, "For we are not fighting against people made of flesh and blood, but against the evil rulers and authorities of the unseen world, against those mighty powers of darkness who rule this world, and against wicked spirits in the heavenly realms" (NLT). Our minds are attacked by the enemy and his evil spirits, and he tries to make it become our obstacle. Our minds seem to have a built in rewind button that keeps replaying what we would like to forget. We re-live past hurt, setbacks and disappointments. A giant can take any shape or form, and it tries to keep us from living the peaceful life God wants us to live. The thing to remember is—no matter what form it takes, or how big it might seem—we should not give any problem more power over us, than God. We must pray and ask God for strength and courage to stand firm and defeat any "Goliath" in our lives.

Prayer for Courage

Father God, I thank You for Your love and faithfulness. Lord, I come to You asking that You grant me the ability to stand firm against the fiery darts of the evil one. I ask that You help me to recognize that I have You as the source of my strength, all I must do is stretch my faith and believe in Your promise. Lord, I know that You do not give us a spirit of fear but of power, love and a sound mind (NKJV). Father, I ask that You give me the confidence I need to face any situation I may encounter because I know that You are with me. In Your son Jesus' name, Amen.

CHAPTER 2

LEAVING HOME FULLY DRESSED FOR BATTLE

Putting on the Armor and leaving home prepared

We have to know that we are in for a fight here on earth. Satan and his evil demons are hard at work to steal souls and wreak havoc on as many lives as they can. Satan's mission is to kill, steal and destroy— just as the Philistines and Goliath wanted to destroy the Israelites. Like David, we have to arm ourselves to be ready for Satan's attacks and schemes. We may not have to do battle with a Philistine army, but Satan is ready to cause confusion in your marriage, give you an unfair boss at work, or drain your bank accounts with unforeseen expenses. He is ready to use whatever he can to get your mind upset and wrapped up in your circumstances so that you will take your mind and eyes off God. If he can accomplish that, Satan is happy.

We have to cover ourselves with the whole armor of God every day. As I mentioned earlier, in Ephesians 6, we are warned that we are not at battle with flesh and blood but with wicked spirits of the unseen realms. In this same chapter, Paul reminds us of how we should fully dress ourselves every day to repel these attacks. In verses 13-17, Paul tells what we should wear: a belt of truth, breastplate of righteousness, shoes of peace, shield of faith, helmet of salvation, and the sword of the Spirit (KJV).

Think of it this way, "Would you leave home in shorts and a t-shirt in snowy, twenty degree weather?" No, of course you wouldn't! You would put on a sweater, pants, boots, scarf and gloves. You would probably even have on layers of clothes. So, "why should we leave home not fully dressed for a spiritual warfare that's going on around us day in and day out?" When we wake in the morning we need to start covering ourselves with our spiritual armor. This needs to happen first thing in the morning–before you even think about your morning coffee. When you wake up, start by spending time with God before going about your daily life.

We can read the word of God and pray before our usual routines of getting ready for work, school or starting the day at home looking after the kids. We need prayer to prepare us for the unknowns a new day brings. Sometimes we even have to pray that our minds are kept right so that we can keep our focus in prayer. You have to prepare when it comes to the enemy's attacks and tricks, so that you might be able to stand against Satan's assaults and your Goliaths.

Prayer for Preparation

Father God, El Shaddai mighty sufficient one. I thank You for Your ever loving grace. Father I ask that You prepare me mentally and spiritually and clothe me in Your protective armor. I ask that You keep me aware of the spiritual battle going on around me every day, for we do not wrestle with flesh and blood but with evil powers of the unseen world. You are the mighty sufficient one, and without You I am not able to do anything. I pray that You keep me alert and covered, Lord.

In Your son Jesus' name, Amen.

CHAPTER 3

WAIST TIGHTENED WITH THE BELT OF TRUTH

The Belt of Truth

First, the belt of truth should be girded around our waists at all times. We have to remember that Paul was writing to Ephesus while he was a prisoner in Rome around A.D. 60. In those ancient times, Roman soldiers would wear these items when going to war. The belt was placed around the waist to aid in holding together armor and keeping it in place. It is also provided a place to carry the sword. If it was large enough, it would also protect vital organs. When you think of a belt, you think of it circling your body and,– going around you. The truth Paul is speaking of is the Word of God. If you do not know the Word of God, then you will be vulnerable to the deceptive lies of the devil. Satan is the great deceiver. This is what Jesus Christ says about Satan in John 8:44, "He was a murderer from the beginning, and abode not in the truth, because there is no truth in him. When he speaketh a lie, he speaketh of his own: for he is a liar, and the father of it" (KJV). We have to read and study the Word of God and develop a relationship with God through the acceptance of Christ as Savior to know the truth.

From the very beginning, when David was chosen by God to be anointed the next King of Israel, God said he looked at a person's thoughts and intentions. He made it known to Samuel that he was well pleased with whom David was on the inside. David had to have had a relationship with God in order for God to be well pleased with him. David's relationship with God and the Holy Spirit living within him allowed him to have confidence in God. David knew the truth about God's greatness and power from reading, hearing and being taught about Him. David's faith grew out of that developing relationship.

Just as David received the Holy Spirit the day he was anointed, we also receive the same Holy Spirit when we accept Jesus Christ. This acceptance and faith is the foundation of believing in the truth of His word because we will now have the Holy Spirit living within us. We become a new creation. "Therefore, if anyone is in Christ, he is a new creation; old things have passed away; behold, all things have become new" (2 Corinthians 5: 17 NKJV). This new creation or new person we have become is one that is filled with the Holy Spirit. Once we accept Jesus Christ as our Lord and Savior the Holy Spirit, our helper and guide that communicates with God, comes to live within us. When you read and study the word of God, meditate on it day and night, you will grow spiritually and become stronger. You will be prepared. The devil is a deceiver, and he tries to destroy that inner spirit connection and communication with God. Satan uses deceit and lies as a way in to kill, steal and destroy that linking your inner spirit man has with the Holy Spirit—Satan wants to make you doubt the truth about God. For example, I grew up telling myself I was too shy and too scared to get up and speak in front of people. I didn't talk much at home. I was afraid to speak in school and even in church. My stomach would hurt from nervousness; my voice would tremble as I spoke. I would be completely terrified! I knew the answers and had great things to say, but I was too afraid to say them. This was a lie of the enemy.

Often our mindset and the way we look at the situation will lead us to believe that we have already failed before we have even gotten started. I was allowing the devil to get into my mind and use what I considered my weakness as a scare tactic to keep me from being God's best. As I got older, I started pushing myself and stepping out of my comfort zone by being in different school activities, competitions and church functions. I did not like feeling threatened by a crowd of people, but I was determined that I was going to overcome this overwhelming anxiety. By giving into this giant in my life, I was causing it to grow bigger and bigger.

Our problems may seem huge to us, but the Bible has an answer to our wrong thinking. I figured out that I needed to take the necessary steps toward victory, but I couldn't do it alone. I started reading and studying the Word of God more, and I was led to this truth. 2 Timothy 1:7: "For God hath not given us the spirit of fear; but of power, and of love, and of a sound mind" (KJV). Not only does God not give us a spirit of fear, but Philippians 4:13 says, "I can do all things through Christ who strengthens me" (NKJV). So, what I was feeling wasn't from God, nor was it a part of the Holy Spirit. Therefore, if fear isn't from God and the Holy Spirit, then how can it be a part of me?

As I mentioned earlier, Scripture says that as a believer of Christ I received the Holy Spirit and became a new creation. Because the Holy Spirit abides in me the spirit of fear does not. Knowing God's word and His promises is the belt of truth that allows us to be able to discern between truth and a lie. It also gives us the courage we need to defeat anything and be victorious. David knew the truth of how mighty God was, and this confidence in the God he served led him to stand boldly against Goliath. He made the truth known to Goliath— the LORD Almighty was so powerful that He didn't need weapons to rescue His people. The truth was that it was the LORD's battle and He would defeat Goliath.

When you know the truth of how mighty your God is, there is nothing the enemy can do to defeat you! Even when the lies of the enemy come disguised as negative thoughts— and then these thoughts are replayed over and over again in your mind. When we tell ourselves, "I'll never get out of debt," or "I will never find the right mate and get married." Or, if you have been through a divorce like myself, you may say, "Has God forgave me, and will I ever find someone to remarry and be happy again?" Every negative thought that comes into our minds should be bound up with our belt of truth and cast down into the pits of hell. These thoughts are not from God. Therefore, they are not true.

When I am attacked by such negativity, I repeat one of my favorite verses: "'For I know the plans I have for you,'" says the LORD. "'They are plans for good and not for disaster, to give you a future and a hope'" (Jeremiah 29: 11 NLT). I am reminded of the truth that I have read and studied. I can be reassured that, "With God all things are possible" (Matthew 19:26 NKJV). We have to stop hitting the rewind button on past thoughts— that suggests pure pessimism. In the end, this will be destructive to our progress of moving forward. Jesus did not go the cross as an atoning sacrifice and die a humiliating death so that we could live a life of defeat! The truth is Satan was defeated when Christ was crucified and resurrected.

If you have accepted this truth and wear it every day you are protected. That belt of truth helps hold every other piece of armor together. David wore his spiritual belt of truth that day against Goliath. David knew how great His God was, and He- would give David victory over the Philistine giant. God did it, allowing victory to come to the Israelites in an unbelievable way. The truth that David knew was put on display for all the rest to see.

Prayer to Put on Your Belt of Truth

Jehovah God, the self-revealing One to those who hunger and thirst after You. Lord, as a deer pants for streams of water (Psalms 42:1 NLT). I ask that You gird my waist with Your belt of truth, keeping all my other armor in place. I know the truth of having the free gift of salvation through the atoning death of Your son Jesus Christ. Lord, you have examined my heart and know everything about me (Psalms 139: 1 NLT), and we already have the victory in any obstacle we face. Any negative thought that says otherwise is a trick of the enemy, for he is a liar. Lord, I ask that as I read Your Word that its truthfulness communicates to my spirit, and it becomes like glue that attaches to my soul. Help me not to leave home without it.

In Your son Jesus' name, Amen.

CHAPTER 4

BREASTPLATE OF RIGHTEOUSNESS

The Breastplate of Righteousness

The second piece of armor Paul advises us to put on is the breastplate of righteousness. First, what is righteousness or being righteous? When you think about being righteous, you think about doing what is right. However, being right from the human standpoint can vary.

When the human nature is involved, there is always a difference in opinion or viewpoint. And those differences can be formulated due to numerous factors: past experiences, beliefs, thoughts, wants or desires. Variations can also be driven by feelings and emotions. The human perspectives on right and wrong cannot be looked upon as being the "supreme" choice or answer. I say this because the human nature is flawed––carnal and fleshly apart from God. So we have to base what is right or righteous on how it is seen through the eyes of God.

God is a Holy God. Therefore, His commandments are righteous and holy; His expectations and standards supersede what we could ever present as our best to Him. Isaiah 64:6 says, "But we are all as an unclean thing, and all our righteousnesses are as filthy rags" (KJV). This being said, we are not made righteous by doing works or from anything we have done or do, because when compared to a Holy God we are still unclean sinners. The only way we are made righteous is by the blood of Jesus Christ when he died as an atoning sacrifice for our sins. 1 John 3: 5-6 says, "And you know that Jesus came to take away our sins, for there is no sin in him. So if we continue to live in him, we won't sin either" (NLT). His death provided us with a way to the Father, and Jesus stands in the gap between our sinful ways and a Holy God.

We should be seeking God's righteousness not our own. If I were to sum up God's standard of righteousness, It would be described as *Christ like.* Christ lived according to God the Father's holy laws and did what was pleasing to the Father. Therefore, if we have the Holy Spirit as our helper living within us as Christians, we too shall be continuing to cultivate a Christ like spirit within us. To be more like Christ should be our ultimate goal. He is our example of true righteousness.

1 John 2:3 says that by obeying His commandments we can be sure that we belong to Him. It doesn't say that each individual person can do his or her own thing as they see right or wrong and still belong to Him. No, we should be seeking to please our Father in heaven by placing His commandments that He created out of love for us in our hearts. When we think of David's most popular used 23rd Psalm, we can see how he knew the importance of God's righteousness. He says, "He leads in the paths of righteousness for His name's sake" (NKJV). Another version reads, "He guides me along right paths, bringing honor to his name" (NLT). It should not only be in our hearts to make the right choices and take the right paths according to God's ways because we love Him and want to show Him honor, but also because it's in our best interest.

I decided to explain righteousness first because it is greatly significant for you to understand what you are to put on. So now, let's go back to discuss the breastplate. Roman soldiers used this piece of armor as protection against fatal blows delivered to their vital organs like the heart and lungs. A wound to the heart or lungs could mean instant death, but a sturdy shield meant an attack in this area would be ineffective. Every blow from the enemy's sword would come in contact with this sturdy metal and, "clang!"–– it would bounce off and not pierce the heart, the most vital organ for all human life. Without the beating of the heart there would be no life.

When the heart is affected, other parts of the body suffer as well. I won't go into much detail about human physiology, but you know the heart pumps the blood which carries oxygen and nutrients throughout the body. When there is no pumping at all there is physical death! This is also true in spiritual death. Our hearts are susceptible to the piercings of this world's evil and wicked ways. We must shield it with not just any breastplate but one that is of righteousness. The righteousness of God should be our covering over the most vital organ in our body. As believers of Christ, we have His righteousness shielding us, guiding our paths and working through us.

We were justified and made righteous in God's eyes by Jesus Christ, and it is our Christian duty to want to do what is right. This protective garment is given as a gift to help us. It keeps our hearts protected–– and therefore, healthy and strong in the LORD. The life-line through which all life flows should not be tainted with evil. If it is, we shall die spiritually, which would be detrimental in having a spirit-guided relationship with God.

"Little children, let no one deceive you. Whoever practices righteousness is righteous, as he is righteous. Whoever makes practice of sinning is of the devil, for the devil has been sinning from the beginning. The reason the Son of God appeared was to destroy the works of the devil (1 John 3:7-8 ESV)." Living as children of God means a responsibility to practice leaving home covered in our righteousness breastplate.

Prayer for the Breastplate of Your Righteousness

Lord God, I ask that You guard my heart against the evil and wickedness created by the prince of this air, Satan himself. I pray that You equip me with Your Holy Spirit as my guide. Help me to be right with You Father, that I may desire to do what is right in Your eyes. Protect my heart Father and do not let even a seed of wickedness be planted within me so that my heart may never be possessed by it. Help me to remember as I leave my house that in everything I do and say, I want to give honor to You while doing it. And anything that the devil throws at me I will not counteract with a not-so-Christ-like behavior.

In Your son Jesus' name Amen.

CHAPTER 5

PUTTING ON YOUR SPIRITUAL SHOES

Shoes of the preparation of the Gospel of Peace

When Paul named shoes as a piece of spiritual armor, you might think why shoes? You may say, "It is not like the enemy will be aiming for my feet." But Paul is not talking about just any kind of shoes–– he is telling us to put on shoes that basically come from the Gospel of Peace.

I do not think any of us would leave home without putting on shoes. Nor would Roman soldiers go to battle without their shoes or sandals. According to Albert Barnes' Bible Notes, the sandals or shoes worn by the Roman soldiers were often fitted with nails, or armed with spikes. This allowed them to be planted firmly in the ground. It kept them from losing their footing while fighting against their enemies. Nowadays, the majority of the time we wear shoes for style. However, shoes do not just look good with an outfit–– even though I love a cute pair of high heels––but they also protect your feet and prepare you for leaving. They prevent our feet from being cut by rocks, glass and other harmful debris. –– For instance, my father Lenord isn't a Roman soldier, but he works in a production plant around all kinds of heavy equipment. He is required to wear steel toe boots to protect his feet from the possibility of heavy equipment falling and seriously injuring him.

Then, on the other hand, when my nephew Lincoln Lenord was only seventeen months old he grasped why shoes, are used and what they represent. They meant that he could go see the ducks in the park. My nephew loves feeding the ducks. He wakes up first thing in the morning, his cute little voices blurting out the words, "duck, duck!" We can be sitting watching television or talking and he comes out of his room with his shoes. He will sit down beside you and put his foot up on your lap. Then he says, "Shoe, shoe, duck, duck!" After we put his shoes on, he goes to the kitchen and grabs his sack of bread crumbs. (My sister and the rest of our family have to keep bread on hand for him because of his new found love of ducks). So, with his shoes on his feet and his sack of bread crumbs in his hand he is ready to go feed his feathered friends in the park.

The point I want to make with this story is that even a seventeen-month-old toddler has learned to equate putting on shoes to going somewhere. In this case, it is to see his duck friends, but he knows once he gets those shoes on he can go. That is the point Paul was trying to make. He says, "And having shod your feet in preparation [to face the enemy with the firm-footed stability, the promptness, and the readiness produced by the good news] of the Gospel of peace" (Ephesians 6:15 Amplified). Paul is telling us that every day we leave home we should place on our feet special shoes that will keep our feet firmly planted and ready to spread and live by the Gospel of Peace.

The Gospel of Peace he is referring to is the Gospel of Jesus Christ. This is the belief in His virgin birth, His death as an atoning sacrifice for our sins, and His resurrection by the power of the heavenly Father. Christ came so that we may have peace. When He went to the cross He took all the sins of mankind upon himself as the sacrificial Lamb of God. We have peace, knowing that the only thing we have to do is believe in Him. We can walk with authority and not in fear, knowing that despite of what Satan may try to throw at us, Christ has overcome the world. "I have told you these things, so that in Me you may have [perfect] peace and confidence. In the world you have tribulation and trials and distress and frustration; but be of good cheer [take courage, be confident, certain, undaunted]! For I have overcome the world. [I have deprived it of power to harm you and have conquered it for you]" (John 16:33 Amplified).

In John 16:33, Christ makes a statement that should leave all of us worry free when we face difficulties if we are living the Christian life. He died so that we may have the peace of knowing the troubling things we face here on earth are only temporary. We are destined for an eternal life of peace in heaven, which is far greater than our circumstances here on earth. Our present sufferings are not worth comparing with the glory that is to be revealed to us (Romans 8:18 ESV).

We can also live with a peace of mind here on earth by deciding to put on those shoes of peace and walk without worry or anxiety. I have decided that I am determined to put on my shoes of peace every day. Even though some days are more difficult than others, I am striving to walk in such a way that I am a witness for Christ and my lifestyle reflects that I have given him total control over the difficulties I cannot change. We have to turn it over to Him and let Him work it out.

Even though many years had passed after my divorce, I was still being tormented with guilt in my mind. I could go for months without feeling shame, guilt and rejection. But then, there would be times that my mind would be wrestling with these negative emotions day in and day out. I wasn't at peace from the effects of my past. I was allowing the enemy to take what he saw as a weakness and use that against me. He was telling me all kind of lies.

This was a death of a relationship, and I was left with feelings of low self-worth, self-esteem and confusion of who I was in Christ. I was suffering from an identity crisis. I would wonder, "What was wrong with me?" The devil only cared about wreaking my peace of mind. He knows that if my mind is consumed with garbage, then I will take my mind off God and it would weaken our relationship. I also wouldn't be living the Christian life.

As Christians, we should be living a life of victory because Christ has overcome the world–– and not be burdened down by our past mistakes and failures. No one is perfect, so we must remember that once we are forgiven God keeps no record––nor should we. I had to forgive and let go. Once we are delivered we have to continue to walk in that deliverance. Christ says, "Come unto me all who are weary and burdened, and I will give you rest. Take my yoke upon you and learn from me, for I am gentle and humble in heart, and you will find rest for your souls" (Matthew 11: 28-29 NIV). We have to do just that! We have to turn it over to God so that He may give us rest. We cannot do it in our own strength but in His.

One day, with the help of the Holy Spirit I think, I just snapped out of it. I remember being in church and the praise and worship team was singing, "Break Every Chain" by Tasha Cobbs. Bishop Kyle Searcy of Fresh Anointing House of Worship, a profound man of God, said–– God wanted chains to be broken off of our lives. And that today He was going to do that. The Bishop had the prayer team pray over every soul in the church, and I can tell you that the Spirit of God was there with us. I felt the Holy Spirit move in me, and I can say I left church that day feeling as if the heavy chains had literally broken off of me. I humbled myself before God and cried out to Him to help me. I think I even got angry. I was angry not only with the devil but with myself for allowing him to keep my mind chained up and in bondage by replaying the hurts of my past over and over in my head. I made up in my mind that day: I refused to live a defeated life. I said to myself, "If the ones who hurt me can walk around being happy and going on with their lives, then why shouldn't I?" I said to myself, "Karina you are not perfect, you have been hurt and you have done some hurting. And sometimes hurt people will hurt other people. You have to forgive yourself and others and move on." I said, Karina you are a child of the Most High God. You are saved and filled with the Holy Spirit. So, why are you not happy?" At that moment I decided that the Goliath in my life, which was a negative mindset, was slayed. – I am walking in peace. Karina–1, and Satan– 0!

Prayer for Walking in Peace

Lord God, allow me to get up every day professing that I will walk in peace. I ask that when I am given the opportunity to spread the Good News of the Gospel of Peace of Jesus Christ I will do so. Lord, I ask that You give me comfort when I need it in my times of trouble and sorrow. I ask that You protect my mind from the author of confusion and help me to rebuke the lies of the enemy. Lord, help me to walk knowing that if You are for me than who could be against me. (see Romans 8:31) Jesus I thank You for leaving with me Your gift of Peace–– not as the world gives but from You– that will keep me from being troubled and afraid (see John 14:27).

In Jesus' name I pray, Amen.

CHAPTER 6

SHIELD OF FAITH

Shield of Faith

For a Roman soldier to go into battle without a shield would be not be smart thinking at all. To be honest, it could mean death! A shield provided a great deal of protection, and it was a substantial tool for defense. It was large enough for a soldier to protect his body from attacks from the enemy. It was also sturdy enough to deliver vicious blows in a counter attack.

As Christians, we are given a spiritual shield. It is the Shield of Faith. In Ephesians 6:16 it states, "Above all, taking the shield of faith with which you will be able to quench all he fiery darts of the enemy" (NKJV). Paul was giving us the message that, just like the Roman soldier was combating fiery darts, arrows and daggers from the enemy, we as Christians have to combat the devil's spiritual attacks against us. The devil's fiery darts are disguised as feelings of doubt, guilt, shame, and worry. The best way for you to extinguish those attacks delivered by the spiritual hosts of wickedness is for you to have faith in God and His sovereignty. Know that God is in control of it all, and He will work all things together for your good. (see Romans 8:28).

As Christian believers, we must have faith in God and His promises. We are God's "just" people. And the Bible says the "just" shall live by faith (see Hebrews 10:38). Having faith in someone or something involves a great deal of trust. "Now faith is the substance of things hoped for, the evidence of things not seen" (Hebrews 11:1 NKJV). We can't see God but when you think about the evidence of things not seen, God's fingerprints are on those things we can see. Those tangible things are the "substances" we have hoped for in faith. So we have to trust God.

When you decide to trust God, and you study the scriptures, you find nothing but evidence of God's faithfulness. You can trust He will express the same faithfulness to you because God is unfailing, and He does not change. God was faithful to His people during their times of trials but they had faith. That is a key factor to overcoming any obstacle, mountain or giant we may face.

Abraham had faith when God told him to offer his son Isaac as a sacrifice. Daniel had faith when he was threatened and thrown in the lion's den for praying to God when it was decreed unlawful. His friends Shadrach, Meshach and Abed-Nego had faith when faced with being thrown a fiery furnace for refusing to bow down and worship an idol god.

I even think about David and how he had the kind of faith that we should mimic as well. He used his shield of faith to extinguish those fiery darts of lies and taunts from Goliath. He used his shield of faith to block out the taunting and disbelief he received from King Saul, the Israelites and even his own brother! David believed God would give him the ability to do something the entire Israelite army didn't believe David——or themselves——could do. King Saul, who was just as frightened as the rest, told David he was ridiculous to believe he could defeat this Philistine. But David didn't give up; he persisted. And we, too, must persist and not give up. When the odds are stacked against you; when there is no one else to give you an encouraging word—— look to God to provide you with the encouragement you need. David looked to God and then encouraged himself.

When Saul finally gave into David's request, I guess the least he thought he could do was to give David protective armor. Saul took off his own armor to dress David to fight Goliath. He gave him a bronze helmet and a coat of mail. The coat of mail was a protective garment made of interlinking rings or metal plates that sort of looked like metal scales. David was not used to wearing these heavy garments so he took them off. He could not walk in the armor because it was weighing him down. He took off the very garments that were to equip and protect him in battle; he went without them. This showed his faith in knowing that God was on his side.

In life, sometimes we, too, must lay things down and let God have his way. I feel we can kind of look at these garments David laid down from another view. I think they can symbolically represent burdens we carry around every day; ones that we haven't laid down before God. Along with the giants that we may be facing, we can also find ourselves carrying around the negative thoughts of past guilt, wrong decisions, condemnations and shame. If you let them, these heavy burdens will weigh you down and turn into downward spiraling emotions. They grab a hold of your mind, and the fester and become towering giants.

David laid down that heavy armor and went to battle with the most important armor of all: the *Shield of Faith in God*! The only way you can have this protective armor for battle is by reading the word of God and having it become ALIVE in you! Our faith in God and His word grows by having a relationship with Him. Our relationship with God is so very important and requires us to spend time with him in spirit through meditation, worship and praise. All we need to do is just believe in His promises and have faith.

God is a faithful God, and we are blessed by his faithfulness. Deuteronomy 7:9 says, "Know therefore that the LORD your God is God who keeps covenant and steadfast love with those who love him and keep his commandments to a thousand generations" (ESV). Is this not the same faithful God David served––and we serve today–– that Moses spoke of thousands of years ago to the children of Israel? God is the same in the past, present and future. When you go through troubled times or are faced with what seems like the impossible, you must turn to Him. Why? Because you would have that special relationship with Him.

For example, we utilize this same concept with our earthly parents. If you need help with something, whatever it may be, if you have a relationship with your parents it is easier for you to turn to them for assistance and have faith that they will help. But if you have not spoken to your mother or father for many years, or have grown apart for whatever reason, it would be hard or almost impossible to ask them for help because of the broken relationship. You probably would not feel comfortable asking for their assistance. If that relationship can be mended or rebuilt, you do it. So, the same concept applies with our Heavenly Father.

We cannot go through life without a strong personal relationship with God and expect to be completely fulfilled and living our purpose-filled life according to His plan. We need to establish that relationship by spending time reading and meditating on the word and in praise and worship. This time with God builds a relationship that allows you to feel comfortable going to Him first in prayer. It allows you to put your faith and trust in Him.

The scriptures are the spoken word of God, and everything we need to know is right there! All we have to do is have faith and trust in his promises. – We, as Christians, have to use our faith in God to cover us so that we know we already have the victory. This is exactly what David did. David had faith in God–– not only from what he had been taught through his Hebrew heritage of how God's faithfulness to his ancestors– but also from his own experiences with God. David remembered how the Lord had delivered him from being attacked by a bear and a lion while tending to his father's sheep. God allowed him to kill them both, and this recollection allowed him to believe God would also deliver him from Goliath (see 1 Samuel 17:34-37).

You must do the same thing David did: remember God's faithfulness in your past and believe He will provide in your present and future. I can remember this one particular time when I was driving home thinking about how I didn't have any money left over out of my paycheck for gas to go back and forth to work. I had made sure I paid my tithes and bills. I did have some gas in my car. I was thinking, "Lord I have two weeks until next pay day, but there has never been a time where I have been stuck beside the road or without gas to go to work or anywhere. So, I know you will provide."

I told myself I wasn't going to worry about it, because I had faith in God that He was going to make a way just like He had done in the past. I was just turning onto my street when my phone rang; it was my sister Shantavia on the phone. She said, "Hey, do you need any money for anything? I have some extra cash if you need me to help you out until your next pay day." All I could do was laugh––and say, "Thank you Lord."

God is so faithful. There is no limit to what God can do. We need to stop putting limits on what He can do and what He can help us to overcome. If we serve the same God that delivered David from the bear, lion and Goliath; the God that provided Abraham a ram in the bush so he wouldn't have to sacrifice his son Isaac (see Genesis 22); the same God that caused the sun to stand still at the request of Joshua so that the Israelites might defeat the Amorites (see Joshua 10:12-14), then why shouldn't we trust him? And these are just a few of God's recorded acts of faithfulness. So if God can do something that great, then why not believe that this same God with awesome supernatural power can heal your body, repair your finances, send new relationships into your life and even turn you away from that addiction. Whatever you are going through, He can be your deliverer.

In Matthew Chapter 17, Jesus talks to his disciples about having faith––even if it is as small as a mustard seed. In verse 20, Jesus says, "I assure you, even if you had faith as small as a mustard seed you could say to this mountain, 'Move from here to there,' and it would move. Nothing would be impossible" (NLT). Jesus is reassuring us that if our faith is small as a mustard seed, then that's all we need to move any mountain, defeat any giant and calm any storm in our lives. When that small mustard seed of faith is watered by the word of God, the possibilities of what you can do are endless. Then, that seed of faith grows and matures. When our faith grows, we mature as Christians.

When you step out in faith, you will become stronger in your walk with God. You will become strong enough to not let your present circumstances determine your future. Life isn't going to be perfect, and Peter even tells us it is essential to endure many trials (see 1 Peter 1:6). So guard yourself from the fiery darts of the enemy by using your shield of faith.

Faith Test

"These trials are only to test your faith; to show that it is strong and pure. It is being tested as fire tests and purifies gold—and your faith is far more precious to God than mere gold. So, if your faith remains strong after being tried by fiery trials, it will bring you much praise and glory and honor on the day when Jesus Christ is revealed to the whole world." (1 Peter 1: 7 NLT).

Prayer for the Shield of Faith

Heavenly Father, I thank You for Your constant, never-ending mercy, love and faithfulness. I ask that You help me to remember how faithful You were to Your children of Israel, the sons and daughters of Abraham. Remind me that I am also in that lineage of blessings as an adopted child into Your family by the blood of Jesus (see Romans 8:15). Father, help me to guard myself against the fiery darts of the enemy. Help me to put on my shield of faith before leaving home to face the world where the prince of the air dwells. Oh Most Holy God, You said in Your word that we all are given a measure of faith (see Romans 12:3) and at times mine may seem that it is the size of a mere mustard seed. So, Lord, I ask that You help me to water that seed with Your word, so that I may grow in knowing and trusting Your faithfulness.

In Jesus' name I pray, Amen.

CHAPTER 7

HELMET OF SALVATION

The Helmet of Salvation

In war, the helmet of the Roman soldiers was used to protect their heads from receiving any fatal blows from the enemy. The importance of a helmet is still emphasized today, with something as simple as riding a bike or motorcycle. There have been so many bicycling accidents in which lives have been spared due to the proper wearing of a helmet. There have also been tragedies in which lives were lost due to head traumas that could have been avoided if only a helmet were worn.

Since the tricks of the enemy starts in our minds, the helmet is a very vital piece of spiritual armor we have and must use. Paul was advising us not to just put on any helmet, but to arm ourselves with the helmet of salvation.

So, just what does this mean for you and me when facing attacks from Satan, his demons and the goliaths in our lives? To me it means having confidence in knowing that you are victorious in Christ and how Jesus' free gift of salvation promises us eternal life. The first step to defeating the enemy is accepting Jesus Christ as your Lord and Savior. You have to believe and have faith that He is God's son and

He died for your sins. "For by grace you have saved through faith, and that not of yourselves; it is the gift of God, not of works, lest anyone should boast" (Ephesians 2:8-9 NKJV). Your salvation is free of charge because God loves you so much!

John 3:16 says, "For God so loved the world that He gave His only begotten Son that whoever believes in Him should not perish but have everlasting life" (NKJV). If God can love us enough to allow His own son to be sacrificed and die a humiliating death like a criminal, how can we not love Him enough to accept His gift of salvation? When you begin to understand that kind of love in your mind and deep down in your spirit, then you should start to know there is nothing God wouldn't do for you! He can free you from depression; restore your peace and health. If it is a part of His Will it shall be done.

I believe I am in remission from Lupus right now because of the grace of God. I believe that by His grace I do not suffer from any complications to my internal organs. For that, I am so thankful. If it were anything different, I would still love Him because I believe in the promise of eternal life upon which eyes are fixed. But as Christians we have to do more than just read about the Word–– we have to live the Word. You have to have your mind renewed and locked in on believing that you are a child of God.

You are victorious through the blood of Jesus Christ; there is nothing the enemy can tell you to make you think otherwise. That is exactly the victorious thinking and attitude that David had on the inside of him. David spoke with authority because he knew God's sovereignty and his power as His chosen people.–– He asked the men in 1 Samuel 17: 26, "For who is this uncircumcised Philistine, that he should defy the armies of the living God" (NKJV)? The boldness in which David spoke that day came from wearing his helmet of salvation. He knew that although Goliath was enormous he still wasn't more powerful than him. He wasn't even circumcised!

Circumcision was a sign of God's everlasting covenant between Him and His people that He made with Abraham and his future descendants (see Genesis 17:10- 14). David knew, as a descendant of Abraham, the authority he possessed. He used that boldness to approach Goliath, a pagan who didn't serve Almighty God and had no authority. David was basically saying, "How can this man who has no covenant with my God––who is omnipotent and sovereign–– defeat me!" There was no doubt in David's mind that his covenant and relationship with God meant something. He was sure it meant victory over any sword, spear or javelin that Goliath could have used against him.

I think anyone has experienced times in life when they just knew without a shadow of a doubt that something was true. For instance, you have taken a test paper and have gone ahead and marked the answers you were sure of to save yourself some time before moving on to the ones that required more thinking. Those were the answers that were certain of; no one, if they wanted to, could change your mind because you just knew you knew! This is exactly how you have to think when it comes to knowing you are saved through the blood of Jesus Christ as an atoning sacrifice and the benefits that come with His death on the cross at Calvary.

David's covenant with God was through his flesh under the old law, but ours comes with accepting Jesus Christ as our Savior. When you accept Christ as your Savior, you are no longer condemned to eternal damnation for your sins–– and you no longer have to fight alone. When the attacks of the enemy come against us, we can have confidence in knowing that we have Almighty God on our side fighting our battles for us (see Joshua 23:10). We can be assured that when we start to feel condemnation for our sins that those feelings are not from God but Satan himself. Christ came into this world so that you and I might be saved not condemned (see John 3:17).

You are no longer condemned to an eternal death due to your sins and transgressions. And although we are still sinners we are justified by the blood of Christ and saved from the wrath of God through Jesus (see Romans 5:8-10). God sends His Holy Spirit to aid us in time of trouble and comfort us in time of need. When you put your attention on God, and the fact that you are not alone and there is eternal life after suffering here on earth, you should have hope. The understanding of His love and free gift of salvation should also give you the desire to want to honor and obey God.

The enemy is not pleased when you accept Christ in your heart and become knowledgeable of the benefits of having a savior. He will do whatever he can to kill, steal and destroy!

To retain information for any academic test you have to study for it. You must do the same to prepare yourself for any test or trial the enemy throws at you by meditating and studying the word. This will give you your helmet of salvation to wear daily to remind you there is hope that is made available through Christ for eternal salvation in the kingdom of God and outweighs the despair you may see before you. It will also protect your mind against being tormented by the struggles that you may face in this world. Do your part and equip yourself to pass the tests!

Prayer for Mental Preparation and Protection

Father God, I thank You for Your everlasting, unconditional love. I can never thank You enough for sending Your Son to die for me and my sins so that I may have eternal salvation with You God. Lord, cause me to hunger after Your word so that I may partake of it as if it were my daily bread. Lord, allow me to be a doer of the word and walk boldly knowing who I am in Christ in spite of what the enemy throws at me. Help me to prepare and protect my mind for spiritual battle by shielding it with the knowledge that I have the power of Jesus Christ within me. Today, Lord, help me to realize the strength and authority I have over the enemy–– and that he does not have it over me.

In Jesus' name, Amen.

CHAPTER 8

SWORD OF THE SPIRIT

The Sword of the Spirit which is the Word of God

The Roman soldiers went to battle fully dressed: belt, shoes, breastplate, shield, and helmet. However, although fully clothed, they would never go out to fight without a weapon! Full body armor was worn for protection from attacks from the enemy, but without a sword as a weapon how would they counter that attack? The soldiers used swords that were sharpened on both edges with a sharp, tapered pointed end. Its sharp, dual edges made it a very versatile and deadly weapon to slay the foes in close-up battle.

When Paul used this analogy of how to be dress for spiritual warfare, he didn't leave out a weapon. The last piece of armor that Paul advised Christians to arm themselves with was a sword. He was speaking of not just any sword, but the Word of God. This was actually the only spiritual weapon Paul told us that we need. All the others were used as armor to cover ourselves. The weapon of choice you as a Christian need to fight the enemy in the spirit is a sharp, double-edged sword. The sword of the spirit can also allow us to see ourselves for who we really are and to allow the corrections we may need.

Hebrews 4: 12 says, "For the word of God is living and powerful, and sharper than any two-edged sword, piercing even to the division of soul and spirit, and of joints and marrow, and is a discerner of the thoughts and intents of the heart" (NKJV). So, this tells us that we, as Christians, must fight back even if the giant we are facing is the one looking back at us in the mirror. It is our responsibility to first search ourselves and get in line with God's Word. Then, we can become fully equipped to stand strong against any enemy's attack and begin to speak the Word of God to every giant, mountain or situation we may face.

Looking back at the story of David and Goliath, David did more than just face this giant with an act of bravery and faith. He faced a Philistine that represented an entire army with God on his side. Before David ran to the battle line to meet Goliath, he spoke to Goliath. He used the name of God as a representation of His faith. David told Goliath that he came to fight him in the name of the LORD of hosts, the God of Israel. He spoke boldly and with confidence, telling Goliath that the LORD would deliver him into his hands (see 1 Samuel 17:45-46).

If we only could have seen what was taking place spiritually when David used God's name. It gave him authority. It gave him victory! This battle was the LORD's to fight. When David put God in the middle of the battle by speaking His name with such faith the sword of the Spirit had already cut Goliath's head off! This happened in the spirit before Goliath was hit with the rock or his head was actually cut off in the natural by his own sword.

You must do the same thing when it comes to fighting battles. As a Christian, not only do you have the Word of God but you also have the name of Jesus to use as your weapon. They work together to create an invincible force to combat the works of the enemy. John 1:1-2 says, "In the beginning was the Word, and the Word was with God, and the Word was God. He was in the beginning with God" (NKJV). The "He" John was referring to was Jesus Christ. The Word of God became flesh to save us from our sins and to give us victory over Satan.

Even Jesus Christ, the son of God himself, had to use the Word of God to counteract the mental attacks of Satan. –In Matthew 4, Jesus had been fasting for forty days and forty nights, and He had become hungry. Sometimes when you are at your weakest moment you are tempted by Satan. When the devil tried to get Jesus to command stones to become bread Jesus told him, "It is written, Man shall not live by bread alone, but by every word that proceeds by the mouth of God (verse 4 NKJV). Jesus was tempted two more times by Satan while in the wilderness, but every time Jesus was tempted He answered with the Word of God. The devil then fled from Him. This is the same way we have to learn to fight.

When we are faced with trials and tribulations, the devil can try to use that to get us to sin against God. Those overdue bills can become all you think about and before you know it they are your focus and not God. They, therefore, become a Goliath tormenting you. The trick of the enemy can even come disguised as alcohol a drug of choice that tells you it will help you forget your frustrations from financial problems, or numb you from the painful feelings of guilt from past sins. However, like Jesus you have to speak the Word of God over your life. Tell yourself, "It is written, I shall lend and not borrow. I am the head and not the tail; I shall be above and not beneath" (see Deuteronomy 28:12-13). These are the promises of God, but you must do your part by living in obedience to His Word and commandments. God will bless you for your obedience.

There have been so many times in my life that I had to speak God's Word over my life. I had to speak words of encouragement in discouraging situations. I can remember that July day in 2009 when I first heard the doctor say, "You have Lupus." I can recall driving home in silence thinking "I am only 26 years old and I could die." I was allowing my mind to think the absolute worst case scenario. I literally thought this was a death sentence. I thought, "Lord why me and why now?" I was still emotionally worn and dealing with so much pain from finalizing my divorce a month prior. I was mentally and physically beat down. I just felt like everywhere I turned the walls were closing in on me. Now, the deteriorating of my health was one more thing to add to my plate. I felt broken, hopeless, and helpless.

I can remember returning to my mother in tears. I could barely get the words out of my mouth through all the sobbing, "I have Lupus."

My mother Rosemary is, at times very straight forward with her words; at this moment, now that I look back on it, I really needed that. She looked straight into my teary eyes and she said, "Karina, where is your faith?" I knew it wasn't a question meant to be answered, but instead a wake up kind of moment. She told me to trust in God.

I was raised to love the Lord, and being a Christian is based on faith and trusting God with every area of our lives. At that very moment something connected in my spirit. I can't say I haven't experienced times of doubt since that day, because your mind will always play that rewind button, but when those doubts and negativity try to creep into my mind I combat them with the Word of God. Proverbs 3: 5-6 says, "Trust in the Lord with all your heart and lean not to your own understanding; but in all your ways acknowledge Him, and He shall direct your paths" (NKJV). This was a trusting kind of God moment, because I did not understand why I was experiencing all of this and I surely didn't know what this meant for me in the future. I did know that God does not make any mistakes and all things work together for good for those that love him (see Romans 8:28).

My faith was not only being tested, but it was being increased. The strength I needed that day and every day since is pulled from the Lord. "As your days, so shall your strength be. There is no one like God, who rides the heavens to help you (see Deuteronomy 33:25-26). This is a favorite sword of mine that I use to cut away doubt, anxiety, exhaustion or whatever weakness I face. I trust in Him to give me just enough strength for each day to be victorious.

Prayer to Persevere with the Word of God

Father God, creator of all things and from which all my blessings flow, I thank you for Your love and kindness and Your son, my Lord and Savior Jesus Christ. I pray that whenever I am faced with troubles and hard times that I remember to use Your word as a tool, a weapon, to fight through anything that is not of You sent to do me harm from the evil one. I pray that as I read Your words, Lord, that they become personified and jump off the pages and become alive in my spirit.

And when my paths become dark, murky and covered with weeds of doubt, I ask that You allow me to remember to use Your word to guide my way and to cut down those weeds of doubt and despair. Lord, You promised in Psalms 119: 105: "Your word is a lamp to my feet and a light to my path" (NKJV). I pray that You help me to hold all things true from You in my heart, and that by prayer and supplication I remain strong.

In Jesus' name, Amen.

CHAPTER 9

SEEING THROUGH THE EYES OF GOD

Seeing through the eyes of God

Seeing through the eyes of our Creator is not something we can always do when we are in the middle of a storm. When we are going through troubled times, seeing things the way God sees them is sometimes the farthest thing from our radar. It is also the hardest thing to do; it is not something we can do on our own. To see things as God sees them simply means to take biblical principles, wisdom and the promises of God as He has it written and then apply them to our lives daily.

God allowed various stories–– from heartache to triumph–– to be recorded in the Bible to give us a point of reference for who He is. We are able to go to the Bible to read about how God showed up in the lives of people just like you and me. This enables us to see examples of His character, faithfulness, as well as the unconditional love of our savior Jesus Christ. However, you must invest in spending time reading and meditating on the Word of God. It takes time, study and preparation by the Holy Spirit to be able to see things how God sees them.

Imagine yourself looking through a telescope into outer space. You want to see the constellation of stars such as The Milky Way or

The Big and Littler Dipper. How do you make out what you are seeing? To the untrained eye, these stars probably just look like a bunch of twinkling lights. However, an astronomer or someone with a trained eye, will be able to look at these formations and be able to distinguish just what they are seeing. In no time they are probably able to point out The Big and Little Dipper, but for those of us who have spent no time learning the science of astronomy it is all foreign to us.

I think it's the same way when you basically learn how to do anything. When you want to take an interest in something to become good enough to become a subject matter expert, you spend time studying it, meditating on it and just absorbing all there is to know about that craft. In the same way, we can spend countless hours talking to that new special someone in our lives trying to get to know them better. How much more should we take in learning and loving on God? We should take the time to study the Bible from Genesis to Revelations. Read God's promises and how much he loves us. If you read Ephesians 2:10, you will learn how God views each of us. Through God's eyes we are His workmanship created in Christ Jesus. We are all crafted carefully in the likeness of His Son. In God's eyes, we are all special. Each and every one of us is carefully made by Him with a purpose and plan here on earth. So, no matter how depressed or low your self-esteem may get; just know that you have a Father in heaven that sees you as a masterpiece. You were crafted by the master craftsman, God Himself! And once you know who you are in Christ and how special you are, there is no obstacle too big for you to handle or overcome.

In Chapter 6 of the book of Judges, is another one of my favorite Biblical stories. It is about an Israelite warrior by the name of Gideon. Gideon was chosen by God to deliver the Israelites from the oppression of the Midianites. They were living in such bondage because of their disobedience. They hid in caves, mountains or dens they had made for themselves so that their enemies wouldn't find them. Whatever they raised, sowed or produced the Midianites, Amalekites and others would come in from the East and take from them. The land was destroyed and barren. The Israelites were constantly tortured, starved and ridiculed. So, they began to cry out to God.

We all have felt, at some point in our lives, something like an Amalekite or a Midianite has come in from the East and taken things from us. Sometimes you may be in such a bad place that it feels like you are not only being attacked from the East but the East, West, North and South–– all at the same time! It didn't matter where you were hiding; you were still vulnerable to the attack.

So, what are you crying out to God for? No matter what you think you may be hiding in your life–– that drug addiction you think no one knows about; the drinking to self-medicate the feelings of guilt from past failures; the lack of self-esteem you may have buried on the inside because of something that happened to you in your childhood. You have to come out from amongst the shadows of your hiding place and cry out to God like the Israelites! You need God to show up in a mighty way to deliver you from the hand of sickness; pull you from under those mountains of bills that keep you down in debt; or maybe resentment about the things that meant the most to you that have been taken away–– precious time with family, health or years of missed opportunities taken by the enemy.

Whether the giants in your life are because of disobedience or to get your attention that you are treading off the directed path for your life, they can leave you crying out to God. There was one time in my life, that when I look back now, I feel like all I did was cry out to God. I was in so much emotional pain that it affected me physically as well. I was going through depression from the ups and downs in my marriage that led to a divorce and at the time I was so embarrassed to talk about it. My body had taken such a beat down from stress that I would stay off work for days at a time lying in bed crying and wondering what I had done so wrong. I felt as if I had been placed on a "naughty list."

I am convinced that all the stress my body had gone through mentally and physically led to the breakdown of my immune system and to my diagnosis of Lupus only one month after my divorce was final. I can remember lying in bed for five days straight with low grade fevers, joint pains and severe fatigue, not knowing what was going on with me. I was separated from family in another state and had no one near but the Lord to cry out to for comfort. Thank God, He heard me and sent my loving parents to care for me. The love of my heavenly Father extends to the hearts of my earthly parents, and I will never forget that kind of love.

My Midianites and Amalekites were a new found illness and the emotional baggage, financial hardship, negative mentality I was carrying from a failed marriage. I was lost and felt so damaged, hurt and alone. In my eyes, I was being punished because the enemy was tricking me to believe that God would not forgive me for getting a divorce. I had a really hard time with that thought and not wanting to disappoint God.

Today, I am victorious over those giants in my life. I may still have the diagnosis of Lupus, but I am blessed to not have any internal organ involvement. I am still believing in God that I never will. I learned to read, pray and spend time alone getting to know God better. I knew growing up that you should pray and ask God for forgiveness, but it wasn't until I really needed his grace and mercy during the lows of my life that I really found out about His unconditional love. Then I learned what grace and mercy were all about. I now know that I had not done anything so wrong, nor had I been placed on a naughty list. Sometimes you have to go through growing pains and have your faith tested. The hard knocks of life are meant to be looked at spiritually, and with your spiritual eyes, see what you can learn and take from those trials.

I had to mediate on what I already knew. I knew God loved me enough to send His son to die so that I might be saved and given eternal salvation. And Jesus Christ loved me enough to sacrifice His own life so that I could have a way to commune with the Father and be made righteous in His eyes. I guess how I thought about this was only on the surface before; but I really had to allow the idea of this love to soak into my mind and be absorbed deep down within my spirit. My mind was full of a lot of false guilt, and the spirit of rejection was weighing heavily on my inner spirit.

One day, I found that Jesus gives you true rest, and I defeated those giants by turning it over to him.

*Come unto Me, all ye that labour and are heavy
laden, and I will give you rest. Take my yoke upon*

you, and learn of me; for I am meek and lowly in heart: and ye shall find rest unto your souls Matthew 11: 28-30 (KJV).

God sees what we think of as misfortunes as opportunities to grow in our faith, a learning experience or a way to show His sovereignty. God wants us to do what we can do in the natural so He can do the rest in the supernatural. It is never God's plan leave us in the midst of our struggles. It is always an opportunity for us to come out victorious.

For example, Gideon became a warrior at the end of the story, but that is not how the story began and definitely not how he saw himself. The Angel of the Lord came to Gideon while he was in his most vulnerable state–– hiding, from the enemy in the winepress while threshing wheat. He spoke to him and called him a mighty man of valor and told him that He would be with him (Judges 6: 13). The Lord had chosen Gideon to deliver Israel from the oppression of the Midianites. Gideon basically told the Lord that he didn't think he was capable of completing such a task because he was from the weakest family of the tribe of Manasseh. He didn't just stop there with his skepticism. Gideon even saw himself as the weakest and least capable in his father's house.

This shows us that sometimes we can be our own worst enemy. You can be the only giant standing in your way of greatness. God's eyes saw Gideon's inner strength, humble spirit, and his potential to lead and to become great. God likes to take what we see in our natural eyes as human beings as not good enough, least favorite, inadequate or impossible and turn it into something great. God's way of using who He considers the right people allows His authority and power to shine through that individual. When Gideon went on to succeed against the Midianites the people of Israel knew God had to be with him. The glory and credit all belonged to God. David, Gideon and all of us are God's vessels for doing His good work. This is how God operates. Therefore, we must remember to give Him reverence in everything because He deserves all the glory and honor.

CHAPTER 10

GET A NEW MINDSET

Renew your mind

To renew our minds means that we are to forget about the troubles of our past—to, not replay those heartbreaking memories in our minds. We should think fresh and new every day. You have to change how you think. Every negative thought that rises up in you that you know is not of God, should be cast down and rebuked in the name of Jesus. You have to get into agreement with God and His word.

Do not allow the enemy to poison your mind with thoughts of failure and despair. You need to think and begin to live like you know the Holy Spirit is living on the inside of you. You have to walk and think with confidence that you can overcome any obstacle and come out victorious. When I think about mind renewing, I think about how the Israelites were freed by Moses, anointed by God, and taken out of the land of Egypt (see Exodus 7:7; 12:40-41). They had been Hebrew slaves for 400 years. God had given a promise many years prior, to their Father Abraham, of how their land would be like no other. They would be free in a land with unlimited potential (see Genesis 12).

However, God allowed them to go through the wilderness for forty years as a period of testing and humbling before they reached their promised land. The Israelites faith grew weak in the testing in the wilderness, so they complained, wanting to go back to Egypt and be slaves. This is a prime example of how not letting go of the past will hinder you and could keep you from having a better future. They wanted to go back to what they knew wasn't good for them because they had lost focus in what God had promised.

Do not allow yourself to keep an "Egypt" mentality when things get tough. Let go of your past failures, leave that "I can't do better than Egypt" way of thinking behind and focus on God while in your wilderness. They failed to change their mindset. Do not make that same mistake.

When Paul was writing to the church of Ephesus explaining the purpose and nature of the church, he also explained how we are to live as children of the light of Jesus Christ. He told them there must be spiritual renewal of thoughts and mind––and this should be done daily (see Ephesians 4:23).

The message Paul gave Ephesus thousands of years ago is the same message we are to use and apply to our lives today. We cannot allow ourselves to become our own worst enemies! We have to know who we are in Christ, and that we are more than a conqueror through the love of Christ (see Romans 8:31 NKJV). We have to have faith in the promises of God and believe that the blood of Jesus covered it all. By his stripes we are healed, forgiven and saved.

Jesus walked this very earth, and He experienced trials and tribulations even before dying on the cross. He was tempted by the devil just as we all have been. So, if no one else understands you can be rest assured that Jesus does. He knows pain, sorrow, and heartache. He even felt like He was separated from God, His own Father when He hung on the cross. Haven't we all experienced at some point a feeling of separation from God? You felt like God wasn't hearing your prayers; but the word of God says, "When the righteous cry for help, the LORD hears and delivers them out of all their troubles (Psalms 34:17 ESV). You may have prayed for a new job, a promotion at work or an increase in your finances but until that blessing comes get in line with the word of God. Be obedient, think positive thoughts, and have faith in God's promises. And while you wait, be content with what you have, for He said, "I will never leave you nor forsake you" (Hebrews 13:5 ESV). He will supply all your needs. (see Philippians 4:19) God has a promise and answer for every one of our needs. We may not be able to change our situation as quickly as we would like, but we can change how we look at the situation.

We can change our minds to think in such a way that is pleasing to God and is ultimately better for our well-being. This makes me think of the time when I had to attend a meeting for prior drug users for an Addictions Counseling class I was taking. I can remember the members expressed how getting in touch with their spirituality and getting to know God had brought them so far, and they are now able to find laughter in light of their past situations. Everyone agreed that when they first started going to the meetings that they felt they were so broken, and their life was so messed up, that they didn't have anything to laugh about.

One individual who spoke said that the first step to recovery was admitting that he had a drug problem. This is a prime example of getting a new mind-set. Not only did they have to change their behavior but they had to also change their thinking. They admitted that they had to change how they looked at their drug use. It was negatively impacting their lives, and it wasn't the life that God wanted them to live. One person's revelation came when "It finally clicked in their head, why am I paying this drug dealer my money for something that makes me crazy?"

I was like, wow, what a revelation. I believe with the help of the Holy Spirit, at that very moment this person's mind-set changed. And when their mind changed, their actions and behavior changed. This person has now been clean and sober since 1989 and still attending meetings today.

God is such an awesome God, and He can move in the lives of anyone. The only things we have to do are repent of our sins and renew our minds to get a new outlook on life. You have to arm yourself with God's love in your heart and know all things are possible to overcome because of the sacrificial love of Jesus Christ. You may even need to repeat this verse over and over again to yourself or write it down and put it somewhere you will see it every day––so that you are reminded,

"I can do all things through Christ who strengthens me" (Philippians 4:13 KJV).

That means all things! Whenever you read that verse and hear the word "ALL" you should just be overwhelmed with a sigh of relief because you don't have to face anything on your own. That means through the power and love of Jesus Christ we can overcome any addiction, heartache, illness, temptation, financial issue, or any other giant that we may face in our lives. If it's God's will, it shall be done.

Life just isn't going to be perfect. There may be not so good seasons or great seasons. But we have hope in Jesus because He came to overcome it all. He came to bring us peace so that we won't have to fight these battles or goliaths alone. In John 14: 33, Jesus says, "I have told you these things, so that in me you may have peace. In this world you will have trouble. But take heart! I have overcome the world" (NIV). So he knows the pains and the setbacks, but He promises peace from it all. All we have to do is believe in his promise and in Him. We have the victory through the blood of Jesus that He shed on Calvary for us all. It's a free gift of protection, doesn't cost any money or anything. It just requires you to believe! God doesn't want you to forget how far He has brought you, but He does want you to overcome the pain of your past. Defeating whatever Goliath in your life standing in the way of your peace and joy begins with you! With Christ all things are possible; He gives us the power to overcome.

Printed in the United States
By Bookmasters

Giants can take any shape or form in your life. They can be past hurts of failed relationships, addictions, setbacks from life's disappointments, and even the torment from yourself and your own negative mindset. You can become so overwhelmed by the many problems you have to face by looking at the size of them, and how they seem to tower over you. Goliath was over nine feet tall, and his size intimated the Israelites, except for young David. This book will inspire and motivate you to become like David and take God to battle with you. You will look at your giants in your life as defeated foes. After reading this book, you will feel encouraged and empowered to slay those giants and walk in victory in the name of our Lord and Savior, Jesus Christ.

KARINA CAMILLE DAVIS

is an author, speaker, and lover of God. Her God-given gift in life is to help and encourage people. She hopes that by telling her story of struggle through life's ups and downs, that she can inspire and motivate others to continue pushing forward. Karina has combined her love for the Lord and writing to be a vessel of hope to those that feel hopeless and discouraged. She wants her readers to know that there is a fighter inside each and every one of us, and with God leading the way, all things are possible. Her goal in life is to walk in her God-given purpose. She has accepted her challenges in life as learning lessons to change, grow and to be confident in herself and the woman she has become. She is taking what the enemy meant for evil and destruction and using it for good and the building of the Lord's kingdom.

U.S. $9.95
ISBN 978-1-4908-8138-
5099

WestBow
PRESS
A DIVISION OF THOMAS NELSON
& ZONDERVAN

9 781490 881386